Knock
Jokes

For Kids 5-7 Years Old

Squeaky-Clean Family Fun

by Mary Miler

financial, medical or professional advice. The content within this book has been derived from various sources. Please consult a licensed professional before attempting any techniques outlined in this book.

By reading this document, the reader agrees that under no circumstances is the author responsible for any losses, direct or indirect, that are incurred as a result of the use of information contained within this document, including, but not limited to, errors, omissions, or inaccuracies.

Table Of Contents

Introduction

Hello there! Welcome to one of the best books about jokes you'll ever find. Congratulations for having such fantastic taste in books, by the way. The jokes in this book aren't just any jokes. They are the best kind of jokes and the best kind of jokes are the kind where a door is involved. That's right! The jokes in this book are knock-knock jokes. Everyone likes a good joke, but no one likes any joke more than a knock-knock joke.

We have everything! Jokes about food, because what's funnier than food? We also have jokes about animals, which isn't difficult seeing as they're pretty funny on their own. There are even jokes about something as silly as shoes. Shoes are very silly and it's easy to make jokes about them.

Now before you get started, I won't say, "I hope you enjoy yourself," because I know that you will. Let's go knock on some doors!

Chapter One: Why is There a Banana Knocking on the Door?

Did you know that knock-knock jokes have been popular for a very long time? Knock-knock jokes are not only older than you or me but they're older than your parents and grandparents too. That's pretty nifty, isn't it? They're so great that they've been around since before 1930! If they've been around that long, then they must be cool, right?

1: Knock, knock.

This is the part where you say, "Who's there?"

Banana!

Now you have to say, "Banana who?"

Banana split!

2: Knock, knock.

You know what to say, "Who's there?"

It's broccoli!

"Broccoli who?"

You're so funny; broccoli doesn't have a last name.

3: Knock, knock.

"Who's there?"

Banana!

"Banana who?"

It's banana your business!

4: Knock, knock.

"Who's there?"

Butter!

"Butter who?

You butter be quick about it. I need the bathroom!

5: Knock, knock.

"Who's there?" You're really getting the hang of saying that.

Beef!

"Beef who?"

Beef-ore I get cold can you let me in?

6: Knock, knock.

"Who's there?"

Ice cream.

This time I want you to say, "Whose cream?"

I'll scream if you don't let me in right now!

7: Knock, knock.

"Who's there?"

Donut!

"Donut who?"

Donut open your presents before Christmas. It's bad luck.

8: Knock, knock.

"Who's there?"

Water.

"Water who?"

Water you waiting for? Just let me in!

9: Knock, knock.

"Who's there?"

Ice cream soda!

"Again? Ice cream soda who?"

Ice cream soda people over there can hear me. Am I loud enough?

10: Knock, knock.

"Who's there?"

Eggs.

"Eggs who?"

You know, I'm eggs-tremely disappointed that you don't even remember me.

11: Knock, knock.

"Who's there?"

Lettuce.

You can go back to saying the usual, "Lettuce who?"

Let us in!

12: Knock, knock.

"Who's there?"

Ketchup!

That sounds odd, "Ketchup who?"

If you ketchup with me then I'll tell you!

13: Knock, knock.

Who's there?

Donut.

"Donut who?"

Donut ask me here; it is top secret. Let me in and I will tell you.

14: Knock, knock.

Who's there?

Beets!

I don't like beets. "Beets who?"

Beets me!

15: Knock, knock.

"Who's there?"

Orange.

"Orange who?"

Orange you getting tired of answering the door all the time!

16: Knock, knock.

"Who's there?"

Cheese.

Cheese is nice. Ask what kind of cheese, or you could say, "Cheese who?"

Cheese a nice girl, don't you think?

17: Knock, knock.

"Who's there?"

Olive!

"Olive who?"

Olive next door to you! Don't you remember me?

18: Knock, knock.

"Who's there."

Turnip.

"Turnip who?"

Turnip up and let's get this party started!

19: Knock, knock.

"Who's there?"

Orange!

"Again? Orange who?"

Orange you glad to see me? Please say yes...

20: Knock, knock.

"Who's there?"

Kiwi.

"Kiwi who?"

Kiwi go to the store for some candy?

21: Knock, knock.

"Who's there?"

Quiche!

"Quiche who?"

Can you give me a hug and a quiche?

22: Knock, knock.

"Who's there?"

Figs!

"Figs who?"

Figs your doorbell! I'm tired of knocking all the time.

23: Knock, knock.

"Who's there?"

Olive.

"Wait! Another Olive? Olive who?"

Olive you. Tell me that you love me too.

24: Knock, knock.

"Who's there?"

Loaf!

"Loaf who?"

I loaf bread so much!

25: Knock, knock.

"Who's there?"

Pudding!

"Pudding who?"

I can say from experience that pudding your shoes on before your pants is a bad idea.

26: Knock, knock.

"Who's there?"

Éclair.

"Éclair who?"

I éclair war! Fisticuffs at dawn!

27: Knock, knock.

"Who's there?"

Water.

"Water who?"

You should really water the plants out here before they die.

28: Knock, knock.

"Who's there?"

Pizza!

I love pizza! "Pizza who?"

Can I have a pizza the pie?

29: Knock, knock.

"Who's there?"

Butter again!

"Butter who this time?"

It's butter if you don't know.

30: Knock, knock.

"Who's there?"

Omelet.

"Omelet who?"

Omelet smarter than I look, I promise.

31: Knock, knock.

"Who's there?"

Honeydew!

"Honeydew who?"

Honeydew you know how pretty you look today? Has anyone told you yet?

32: Knock, knock.

"Who's there?"

Hungry clock.

That's not a food but, "Hungry clock who?"

The hungry clock went back four seconds, because the food was just that good.

33: Knock, knock.

"Who's there?"

Pasta!

"Pasta who?"

Pasta food please, I'm starving!

34: Knock, knock.

"Who's there?"

Kale!

"Kale who?"

Looks like you've got some time to kale. Let me in.

35: Knock, knock.

"Who's there?"

Muffin.

"Muffin who?"

Muffin's going on with me. What are you up to?

36: Knock, knock.

"Who's there?"

Egg!

"Egg who?"

I'm egg-cited to meet you, so let me in!

37: Knock, knock.

"Who's there?"

Water.

"Water who?"

Water do you think you're doing in my house and where's my key?

38: Knock, knock.

"Who's there?"

Jellybean.

"Jellybean who?"

Haven't you been paying attention? I just told you I'm Jelly bean!

39: Knock, knock.

"Who's there?"

Lettuce!

"Lettuce who this time?"

Lettuce in and maybe you'll find out.

40: Knock, knock.

"Who's there?"

Banana!

"Banana who?"

Banana!

"Banana who?"

Banana!

"Banana who?" **Knock, knock.**

"Wait! What? Who's there?"

Orange.

"Orange who?"

Orange you glad I didn't say banana! I bet I was making you go bananas.

41: Knock, knock.

"Who's there?"

Pasta!

"Pasta who?"

Pasta la vista, baby!

42: Knock, knock.

"Who's there?"

Water!

"Water who?"

Water you doing today? Can we do something together?

43: Knock, knock.

"Who's there?"

Pecan.

"Pecan who?"

Why don't you pecan somebody your own size!

44: Knock, knock.

"Who's there?"

Pasta.

Not again! "Pasta who?"

Can you pasta salt please?

45: Knock, knock.

"Who's there?"

Turnip.

"Turnip who?"

Turnip the volume of the doorbell, I don't think you heard it ring.

46: Knock, knock.

"Who's there?"

Peas!

"Peas who?"

Peas to meet you!

47: Knock, knock.

"Who's there?"

Butter.

"Butter who?"

Butter bring that umbrella with you; I think it's going to rain.

48: Knock, knock.

"Who's there?"

Orange.

No, not orange again! "Orange who?"

Orange you going to open the door! It's very rude not to.

49: Knock, knock.

"Who's there?"

Banana peeling.

"Banana peeling who?"

Do you know a doctor? My banana is peeling kind of bad.

50: Knock, knock.

"Who's there?"

Cash.

"Cash who?"

No thank you, I prefer peanuts to cashews.

51: Knock, knock.

"Who's there?"

Cereal.

"Cereal who?"

There's a cereal killer on the loose! He threw a whole box of cornflakes on the floor and stepped on them all. Let me in quick!

52: Knock, knock.

"Who's there?"

Honey.

"Honey who?"

Honey, can you open the door for me?

53: Knock, knock.

"Who's there?"

Cabbage!

"Cabbage who?"

How many cabbages do you know that have last names?

54: Knock, knock.

"Who's there?"

Mango!

"Mango who?"

Mango to the door and open it up already! Do you have any idea how long I've been standing here?

55: Knock, knock.

"Who's there?"

Irish stew.

"Irish stew who?"

Irish stew in the name of the law!

56: Knock, knock.

"Who's there?"

Icing.

"Icing who?"

Icing loudly, so you might want to get your earplugs.

57: Knock, knock.

"Who's there?"

Nut.

"Nut who?"

Nut telling you!

58: Knock, knock.

"Who's there?"

Orange.

"Orange who?"

Orange you sick of hearing about oranges!

59: Knock, knock.

"Who's there?"

Egg!

"Egg who?"

Egg-cuse me! That's a very rude way to answer the door.

60: Knock, knock.

"Who's there?"

Butter.

How many butters are there? "Butter who?"

I butter tell you some more knock-knock jokes before you get bored!

61: Knock, knock.

"Who's there?"

Mushroom.

"Mushroom who?"

There isn't mushroom out here! Is it bigger in there?

Chapter Two: Can Animal's Knock on Doors?

The very first knock-knock joke wasn't even a knock-knock joke at all. Way back in time, further than anyone can remember, they were known as "Do you know" jokes. Someone, a joker, a jester, or just a really funny guy, would walk up to someone else on the street and ask them something like, "Do you know Arthur?" Then the person who is unsuspecting of the clever joke they are about to hear responds with, "Arthur who?" Then the joker would yell, "Arthurmometer!" Then he would laugh at the person and run away. That was the start of the knock-knock joke frenzy! That was as far into the past as 1900! I don't know about you but I think there are better jokes now.

1: Knock, knock.

"Who's there?"

Quack.

"Quack who?"

You really quack me up sometimes!

2: Knock, knock.

"Who's there?"

Herd.

"Herd who?"

I herd that you were home. Can I come in and play?

3: Knock, knock.

"Who's there?"

Duck!

"Duck who?"

Donald, Donald Duck, and I like my quakers shaken not stirred.

4: Knock, knock.

"Who's there?"

Owl's say.

"Owl's say who?"

You're right, they do.

5: Knock, knock.

"Who's there?"

Interrupting Cow!

"Interrupting cow—"

MOOOOOOOO!

6: Knock, knock.

"Who's there?"

Rough!

That sounds strange. "Rough who?"

Rough, rough, rough! It's your dog silly, let him in!

7: Knock, knock.

"Who's there?"

Alpaca.

An alpaca here! "Alpaca who?"

Alpaca suitcase and we can go somewhere!

8: Knock, knock.

"Who's there?"

Cows go.

"Cows go who?"

No silly! Cows go 'moo' they don't go 'who'!

9: Knock, knock.

"Who's there?"

Lion!

"Lion who?"

I'm lion on your doorstep because I'm bored! Open the door!

10: Knock, knock.

"Who's there?"

Hoo!

"Hoo who?"

Why are you talking like an owl?

11: Knock, knock.

"Who's there?"

Duck!

"Duck who?"

No just duck! They're throwing eggs at the house!

12: Knock, knock.

"Who's there?"

Yorkie's.

"Yorkie's who?"

Put Yorkie's in the lock and open the door already.

13: Knock, knock.

Who's there?

Wood ant.

"Wood ant who?"

Don't worry, I wood ant hurt a fly. You can let me in now.

14: Knock, knock.

"Who's there?"

Whale!

"Whale who?"

Let me in and we can have a whale of a good time!

15: Knock, knock.

"Who's there?"

Goat.

"Goat who?"

Goat on a limb and open the door for me.

16: Knock, knock.

"Who's there?"

Toucan!

"Toucan who?"

Toucan play at that game! Come and knock on my door just now.

17: Knock, knock.

"Who's there?"

Spider!

"Spider who?"

There's a spider out here, let me in!

18: Knock, knock.

"Who's there?"

Chimp!

"Chimp who?"

Isn't it pronounced shampoo?

19: Knock, knock.

"Who's there?"

Bunny.

"Bunny who?"

Some bunny stole all of my carrots!

20: Knock, knock.

"Who's there?"

Rabbit.

"Rabbit who?"

Rabbit up already. I've got places I need to be.

21: Knock, knock.

"Who's there?"

Who.

"Who who?"

Are you an owl or something?

22: Knock, knock.

"Who's there?"

Oink, oink!

"Oink, oink who?"

Can you make up your mind? You can't be a pig and an owl.

23: Knock, knock.

"Who's there?"

Dino!

"Dino who?"

It's dinosaur not dino who!

24: Knock, knock.

"Who's there?"

Fish!

"Fish who?"

Bless you! But you should really cover your mouth when you sneeze.

25: Knock, knock.

"Who's there?"

Chicken!

"Chicken who?"

I would like to chicken to my room. Isn't this the hotel?

26: Knock, knock.

"Who's there?"

Fangs!

"Fangs who?"

Fangs for letting me know that you were home!

27: Knock, knock.

"Who's there?"

Interrupting Raven.

"Interrupting—"

CAW!

28: Knock, knock.

"Who's there?"

Dragon.

"Dragon who?"

Stop dragon your feet and hurry up and open this door!

29: Knock, knock.

"Who's there?"

Monkey!

"Monkey who?"

You know what they say, 'Monkey see monkey do!'

30: Knock, knock.

"Who's there?"

Herring.

"Herring who?"

I'm herring some really awesome jokes right now!

31: Knock, knock.

"Who's there?"

Halibut!

"Halibut who?"

Halibut opening up this door for me?

32: Knock, knock.

"Who's there?"

Werewolf.

A werewolf! Oh no! Wait it's not a full moon so we should be okay. "Werewolf who?"

Werewolf I find the bathroom? I've really got to go!

33: Knock, knock.

"Who's there?"

Possum!

"Possum who?"

Possum food or something if I'm going to be stuck out here for long.

34: Knock, knock.

"Who's there?"

Bat!

"Bat who?"

I bat you'll never guess who I am!

35: Knock, knock.

"Who's there?"

Howl!

"Howl who?"

Now, howl you now if you won't open the door for me?

36: Knock, knock.

"Who's there?"

Amos.

"Amos who?"

A mosquito!

37: Knock, knock.

"Who's there?"

Honeybee!

"Honeybee who?"

Honeybee a dear and get me some water for these plants out here. They're dying out here!

38: Knock, knock.

"Who's there?"

Chick!

"Chick who?"

You better chick your stove, I think I smell something burning.

39: Knock, knock.

"Who's there?"

Another.

"Another who?"

Another mosquito!

40: Knock, knock.

"Who's there?"

Geese!

"Geese who?"

Geese what I'm going to do if you don't open the door right now!

41: Knock, knock.

"Who's there?"

Bee!

"Bee who?"

You better bee at my house in hive minutes!

42: Knock, knock.

"Who's there?"

Moose!

"Moose who?"

Moose you be so nosey about it?

43: Knock, knock.

"Who's there?"

Iguana!

"Iguana who?"

Iguana come inside, so open the door already!

44: Knock, knock.

"Who's there?"

Aardvark.

"Aardvark who?"

Aardvark a really long way to see you, so can you let me in now?

45: Knock, knock.

"Who's there?"

Yeta.

"Yeta who?"

Yet another mosquito!

46: Knock, knock.

"Who's there?"

Kanga!

"Kanga who?"

Actually, it's kangaroo not kanga-who, thank you very much!

47: Knock, knock.

"Who's there?"

Possum!

"Possum who?"

Possum more water please!

48: Knock, knock.

"Who's there?"

Cod!

"Cod who?"

How cod you say that? I was just here and you don't even remember me!

49: Why did the chicken cross the road? To get to the house!

Knock, knock.

"Who's there?"

THE CHICKEN! Weren't you listening?

50: Knock, knock.

"Who's there?"

Alligator.

"Alligator who?"

Alligator was a card for her birthday. Do you think she'll like it?

51: Knock, knock.

"Who's there?"

Nota.

"Nota who?"

Not another mosquito...

52: Knock, knock.

"Who's there?"

Soup.

"Soup who?"

Soup-er man!

53: Knock, knock.

"Who's there?"

Gorilla!

"Gorilla who?"

Gorilla hamburger for me will you. I'm starving!

54: Knock, knock.

"Who's there?"

Hip.

"Hip who?"

Hippopotamus is my full name but it's quicker if you just call me Hip.

55: Knock, knock.

"Who's there?"

Goose!

"Goose who?"

Goose who's knocking again. It's me, the person you can't remember!

56: Knock, knock.

"Who's there?"

Flea.

"Flea who?"

Flea blind mice climbed up the clock. I don't why.

57: Knock, knock.

"Who's there?"

Cereal.

"Cereal who?"

Cereal pleasure to finally meet up, even if I am talking to a closed door.

58: Knock, knock.

"Who's there?"

Water!

"Water who?"

Water way to answer a door! It seems very rude to be asking so many questions.

59: Knock, knock.

"Who's there?"

Chick!

"Chick who?"

Chick out all of these awesome knock-knock jokes!

Chapter Three: What's in a Name but a Joke!

Some believe that knock-knock jokes were first made popular by a very famous man. You may know him or you may not but you most certainly know about him. William Shakespeare is a very important man. He wrote stories and in those stories you can find a knock-knock joke or two. One of his characters, who is named Macbeth, used to say 'Knock, knock!' and 'Who's there?' all the time.

"Knock, knock! Who's there, I, the name of Beelzebub?"

That's one of the things that Macbeth said. It's not a very funny joke but I'm sure he meant for it to be. Knock-knock jokes have gotten a lot better lately. Wouldn't you agree?

1: Knock, knock.

"Who's there?"

Heidi.

"Heidi who?"

Why did you Heidi key from me?

2: Knock, knock.

"Who's there?"

Alex.

"Alex who?"

Alex-plain that to you when you open the door and let me in!

3: Knock, knock.

"Who's there?"

Nun!

"Nun who?"

It's really nun of your business, is it?

4: Knock, knock.

"Who's there?" Can I just say you're getting really good at saying that?

Oscar.

"Oscar who?"

Well, if you're going to Oscar silly question then I'm going to give you a silly answer.

5: Knock, knock.

"Who's there?"

Anna Partridge!

"Anna Partridge who?"

Anna Partridge in a pear tree. Sing along with me!

6: Knock, knock.

"Who's there?"

Arthur.

"Arthur who?"

Arthur-mometer is what you use to check someone's temperature.

7: Knock, knock.

"Who's there?"

Conrad!

"Conrad who?"

Conrad-ulations! I heard it was your birthday.

8: Knock, knock.

"Who's there?"

Dwayne.

"Dwayne who?"

Dwayne the bathtub quick! I'm drowning in here!

9: Knock, knock.

"Who's there?"

Candice.

"Candice who?"

Candice door even open or am I stuck out here forever?

10: Knock, knock.

"Who's there?"

Billy Bobby Joe Baker.

"Billy Bobby Joe Baker who?"

Seriously? How many Billy Bobby Joe Baker's do you know?

11: Knock, knock.

"Who's there?"

Oswald.

"Oswald who?"

Oswald my gum by accident. Help!

12: Knock, knock.

"Who's there?"

Theodore.

"Theodore who?"

Theodore wasn't open and the doorbell is still broken, so I had to knock.

13: Knock, knock.

"Who's there?"

Kenya!

"Kenya who?"

Kenya open the door already!

14: Knock, knock.

"Who's there?"

Amish.

"Amish who?"

You're a shoe? That's not what I was expecting to hear when I knocked on the door.

15: Knock, knock.

"Who's there?"

Luke!

"Luke who?"

If you'd Luke through the keyhole, then you'd know!

16: Knock, knock.

"Who's there?"

Obi Wan.

"Obi Wan who?"

Really? You know more than one Obi Wan?

17: Knock, knock.

"Who's there?"

Howard.

"Howard who?"

Howard, I know! Just open the door.

18: Knock, knock.

"Who's there?"

Ab.

"Abe who?"

Ab, C, D, E, F, G... don't you know your alphabet?

19: Knock, knock.

"Who's there?"

Nicholas.

"Nicholas who?"

You know a Nicholas not that much money these days. It's not even enough to buy a sweet.

20: Knock, knock.

"Who's there?"

Alma.

"Alma who?"

Alma not going to tell you until you open the door.

21: Knock, knock.

"Who's there?"

Jess.

"Jess who?"

Can you Jess let me in already?

22: Knock, knock.

"Who's there?"

Anita!

"Anita who?"

Anita borrow some sugar and milk or else I can't make a cup of tea.

23: Knock, knock.

"Who's there?"

Gino.

"Gino who?"

Gino who I am. Stop playing around and open the door.

24: Knock, knock.

"Who's there?"

Annie.

"Annie who?"

Isn't Annie body going to open this door! I'm tired of knocking all the time.

25: Knock, knock.

"Who's there?"

Annie again!

"Again? Annie who?"

Annie-thing you can do, I can do better! Admit it, you sang that.

26: Knock, knock.

"Who's there?"

Candice.

"Candice who?"

Candice joke get any better? No, I don't think it can.

27: Knock, knock.

"Who's there?"

Barbara.

"Barbara who?"

Barbara, black sheep have you got any wool with you?

28: Knock, knock.

"Who's there?"

Ben.

"Ben who?"

I've Ben knocking for a long time now can you open up already!

29: Knock, knock.

"Who's there?"

Iva!

"Iva who?"

Iva sore hand from knocking all the time! Get that doorbell fixed.

30: Knock, knock.

"Who's there?"

Abbey.

"Abbey who?"

Abbey stung me on the nose and it hurts.

31: Knock, knock.

"Who's there?"

Abby.

"Abby who?"

Abby birthday to you! I don't know if it's your birthday I just like singing that song.

32: Knock, knock.

"Who's there?"

Al.

"Al who?"

Al give you a big kiss if you open up the door!

33: Knock, knock.

"Who's there?"

Adolph!

"Adolph who?"

Adolph ball hit me on the head and now I have a bump there.

34: Knock, knock.

"Who's there?"

Anna.

"Anna who?"

Anna one, Anna two, Anna three! Open the door for me! You were supposed to open on three.

35: Knock, knock.

"Who's there?"

Ash.

"Ash who?"

Bless you. Now that you're done sneezing can you open up?

36: Knock, knock.

"Who's there?"

Amanda.

"Amanda who?"

Amanda fix the doorbell, let him in.

37: Knock, knock.

"Who's there?"

Barbie!

"Barbie who?"

Funny, I thought there was only one Barbie. Which one do you think this is?

38: Knock, knock.

"Who's there?"

Joe!

"Joe who?"

I like Joe-king around with you.

39: Knock, knock.

"Who's there?"

Doris and Ken.

"Doris and Ken who?"

The Doris locked. Unlock it so we Ken come in.

40: Knock, knock.

"Who's there?"

Stan!

"Stan who?"

Stan-pede! Get out of the way!

41: Knock, knock.

"Who's there?"

Frank.

"Frank who?"

Frank you very much for letting me in. That's what I'm going to say when you finally open the door for me.

42: Knock, knock.

"Who's there?"

Brie.

"Brie who?"

Brie a good neighbor and let me in.

43: Knock, knock.

"Who's there?"

Candice.

"Candice who?"

Candice be the last question you ask me?

44: Knock, knock.

"Who's there?"

Champ!

"Champ who?"

You should Champ-poo your hair, it looks dirty from here.

45: Knock, knock.

"Who's there?"

Colleen.

"Colleen who?"

You should Colleen up this mess.

46: Knock, knock.

"Who's there?"

Dewey.

"Dewey who?"

Dewey have to go through this every time I knock on your door?

47: Knock, knock.

"Who's there?"

Isabel.

"Isabel who?"

Isabel not working still? I had to knock again.

48: Knock, knock.

"Who's there?"

Kent!

"Kent who?"

Kent you tell who I am, or have you forgotten about me already?

49: Knock, knock.

"Who's there?"

Dwayne.

"Dwayne who?"

Dwayne, the knock, Johnson.

50: Knock, knock.

"Who's there?"

Emma!

"Emma who?"

Emma making you laugh with this amazing jokes?

51: Knock, knock.

"Who's there?"

Fillmore.

"Fillmore who?"

Do you Fillmore confident about opening the door yet?

52: Knock, knock.

"Who's there?"

Sherlock.

"Sherlock Holmes! Is that you?"

No! You Sherlock your door tight, don't you?

53: Knock, knock.

"Who's there?"

Annie.

"Annie who?"

Are you going to open this door Annie time soon?

54: Knock, knock.

"Who's there?"

Daisy.

"Daisy who?"

Daisy me rollin' and they're hatin'! I like that song.

55: Knock, knock.

"Who's there?"

Aaron.

"Aaron who?"

Aaron you going to open the door for me?

56: Knock, knock.

"Who's there?"

Andrew.

"Andrew who?"

Andrew a picture just for you. Open the door so I can show it to you.

57: Knock, knock.

"Who's there?"

Gus.

"Gus who?"

Don't you want to try and Gus who?

58: Knock, knock.

"Who's there?"

Hayden.

"Hayden who?"

Hayden seek is my favorite game. Want to play?

59: Knock, knock.

"Who's there?"

Wendy.

"Wendy who?"

Wendy bell works again then I won't have to knock all the time.

60: Knock, knock.

"Who's there?"

Otto.

"Otto who?"

You Otto let me in soon!

61: Knock, knock.

"Who's there?"

Troy.

"Troy who?"

"Troy-d ringing the doorbell, but it didn't work. Knocking doesn't seem to be working either because the door is still closed.

62: Knock, knock.

"Who's there?"

Hugo.

"Hugo who?"

Hugo get the key and I'll wait here patiently.

63: Knock, knock.

"Who's there?"

Tyrone.

"Tyrone who?"

Tyrone shoelaces! I'm busy tying mine.

64: Knock, knock.

"Who's there?"

Howie.

"Howie who?"

I'm fine, thank you for asking. Howie you?

65: Knock, knock.

"Who's there?"

Mikey!

"Mikey who?"

Mikey doesn't want to unlock the door! Did you give me a fake key?

66: Knock, knock.

"Who's there?"

Ike.

"Ike who?"

Ike have no idea!

67: Knock, knock.

"Who's there?"

Lena.

"Lena who?"

If you Lena bit closer to me then I'll tell you, because it's a secret so I have to whisper.

68: Knock, knock.

"Who's there?"

Iris.

"Iris who?"

Iris you didn't ask me that question.

69: Knock, knock.

"Who's there?"

Wendy.

"Wendy who?"

Wendy the bell works then I won't have to knock anymore, because I know you think it's annoying.

70: Knock, knock.

"Who's there?"

Justin!

"Justin who?"

I was Justin the neighborhood, so I thought I'd stop by!

71: Knock, knock.

"Who's there?"

Olive.

"Olive who?"

Olive pizza but I don't like olives on pizza. In fact, I don't like olives at all.

72: Knock, knock.

"Who's there?"

Isaac.

"Isaac who?"

Isaac-ly who do you think you're talking to?

73: Knock, knock.

"Who's there?"

Adore.

"Adore who?"

Adore is made to be answered not kept shut.

74: Knock, knock.

"Who's there?"

Gladys.

"Gladys who?"

Gladys the weekend already.

75: Knock, knock.

"Who's there?"

Justin!

"Justin who?"

I'm Justin time for dinner!

76: Knock, knock.

"Who's there?"

Jewel!

"Jewel who?"

Jewel remember me once you open the door.

77: Knock, knock.

"Who's there?"

Joe.

"Joe who?"

I'm just Joe-king with you.

78: Knock, knock.

"Who's there?"

Ishmael.

"Ishmael who?"

Ishmael something fishy about all these questions.

79: Knock, knock.

"Who's there?"

Juana.

"Juana who?"

Juana open up for me or not.

80: Knock, knock.

"Who's there?"

Ken.

"Ken who?"

Ken you tell me all the really good knock-knock jokes? Oh, wait I already know them all.

81: Knock, knock.

"Who's there?"

Norma Lee.

"Norma Lee who?"

Norma Lee I have my own key but I lost it, so can you let me in?

82: Knock, knock.

"Who's there?"

Gladys.

"Gladys who?"

Gladys you that answered the door. I know you'll let me in.

83: Knock, knock.

"Who's there?"

Aladdin.

"Aladdin who?"

Aladdin the street wants to speak with you about your doorbell.

84: Knock, knock.

"Who's there?"

Alex.

Haven't we already had an Alex knock? "Alex who?"

Hey! Alex the questions around here, buddy!

85: Knock, knock.

"Who's there?"

Bruce.

"Bruce who?"

I Bruce easily so don't hit me!

86: Knock, knock.

"Who's there?"

Robin!

"Robin who?"

You! I'm Robin you. Now give me all your money.

87: Knock, knock.

"Who's there?"

Ishmael.

"Ishmael who?"

Ishmael something good. Are you cooking in there?

88: Knock, knock.

"Who's there?"

Al.

"Al who?"

Al tell you if you let me in.

89: Knock, knock.

"Who's there?"

Lisa.

"Lisa who?"

The Lisa you could do is let me in.

90: Knock, knock.

"Who's there?"

Keanu.

"Keanu who?"

Keanu let me in now. I really want to sit down.

91: Knock, knock.

"Who's there?"

Hugh!

"Hugh who?"

What are Hugh talking about? You know me now let me in.

92: Knock, knock.

"Who's there?"

Scott.

"Scott who?"

Scott nothing to do with you.

93: Knock, knock.

"Who's there?"

Luke.

"Luke who?"

Luke out for some more great jokes up ahead.

94: Knock, knock.

"Who's there?"

Kermit!

"Kermit the frog?"

No.

"Kermit who?"

Kermit a crime and the police will come after you.

95: Knock, knock.

"Who's there?"

Trish.

"Trish who?"

Yes please! My nose is a little runny.

96: Knock, knock.

"Who's there?"

Wayne.

"Wayne who?"

It's Wayne-ing out here! Can you let me in before I get soaked?

97: Knock, knock.

"Who's there?"

Claire!

"Claire who?"

Claire the way because I'm coming through!

98: Knock, knock.

"Who's there?"

Willy.

"Willy who?"

Willy open the door or not? Looks like not.

99: Knock, knock.

"Who's there?"

Goliath.

"Goliath who?"

You should Goliath down. You looketh really tired.

100: Knock, knock.

"Who's there?"

Mary.

"Mary who?"

Mary Christmas!

101: Knock, knock.

"Who's there?"

Abby.

"Abby who?"

Abby New Year!

102: Knock, knock.

"Who's there?"

Juno.

"Juno who?"

Juno exactly who I am, stop messing around!

103: Knock, knock.

"Who's there?"

Conrad.

"Conrad who?"

Conrad-ulations for answering the door so quickly! Now all you have to do is open it.

104: Knock, knock.

"Who's there?"

Robin.

"Robin who?"

Those guys are Robin your house!

105: Knock, knock.

"Who's there?"

You mean you don't even remember my name? I think I'm going to cry.

106: Knock, knock.

"Who's there?"

Harry.

"Harry who?"

Well you Harry up and open the door already!

107: Knock, knock.

"Who's there?"

Nana.

"Nana who?"

I'm sure it's Nana your business!

108: Knock, knock.

"Who's there?"

Keith.

"Keith who?"

Keith me and let me in pleith.

109: Knock, knock.

"Who's there?"

Hammond.

"Hammond who?"

Hammond eggs please. Fry them up and put them on a plate for me.

110: Knock, knock.

"Who's there?"

Hugh.

"Hugh who?"

Why do Hugh have to know?

111: Knock, knock.

"Who's there?"

Buddha.

"Buddha who?"

Buddha some toast and pour some tea. I'm coming in for breakfast.

112: Knock, knock.

"Who's there?"

Ozzie!

"Ozzie who?"

Ozzie you later. I've got to go.

113: Knock, knock.

"Who's there?"

Alec.

"Alec who?"

Alec-tricity was a really shocking discovery!

114: Knock, knock.

"Who's there?"

Caesar!

"Caesar who?"

Caesar quick! Before she gets away!

115: Knock, knock.

"Who's there?"

Cher.

"Cher who?"

Cher would be nice if you would open the door for me.

116: Knock, knock.

"Who's there?"

Annie.

"Annie who?"

Annie other way I can get in or is the door my only option?

117: Knock, knock.

"Who's there?"

Hugh.

"Hugh who?"

I'll have to get back to Hugh on that one.

118: Knock, knock.

"Who's there?"

Earl.

"Earl who?"

Earl be glad when you let me in so I can sit down.

119: Knock, knock.

"Who's there?"

Noah!

"Noah who?"

Do you Noah good place for us to go eat?

120: Knock, knock.

"Who's there?"

Dewey.

"Dewey who?"

Dewey even have a key for this door?

121: Knock, knock.

"Who's there?"

Amma.

"Amma who?"

Amma not going to tell you until you open the door.

122: Knock, knock.

"Who's there?"

Gerald!

"Gerald who?"

Don't you remember me. It's Gerald friend from school.

123: Knock, knock.

"Who's there?"

Britney Spears!

The Britney Spears! It can't be. "Britney Spears who?"

Knock, knock – oops! I did it again.

124: Knock, knock.

"Who's there?"

Phillip!

"Phillip who?"

Phillip my Halloween bag with lots of candy!

125: Knock, knock.

"Who's there?"

Ferdie.

"Ferdie who?"

Ferdie last time can you open the door already!

126: Knock, knock.

"Who's there?"

Will.

"Will who?"

Will you open the door already and let me in! It's cold out here and these plants still need some water!

127: Knock, knock.

"Who's there?"

Frank.

"Frank who?"

Frankenstein, trick or treat!127: Knock, knock.

"Who's there?"

Ivan!

"Ivan who?"

Ivan to suck all of your blood! That's what a vampire would say if I were a vampire, but I'm not.

128: Knock, knock.

"Who's there?"

Diane.

"Diane who?"

I'm Diane out here! Open the door!

Chapter Four: All the Places That will Come to Your Door.

You know how they say that laughter is always the best medicine. Well, they're not wrong! It really is and nothing can make you laugh more than a really good joke. Kind of like the jokes that are right in front of you. Did you know that there's no such thing as a fake laugh? We can fake smile if we're really upset but it's impossible to fake a genuine laugh. You can make a sound that makes everyone think that you're laughing but you can never trick your brain. Your brain knows when you're laughing and when you're not.

1: Knock, knock.

This time I want you to say 'where's there.' You can't ask a place who's there because they're not a who they're a where. "Where's there?"

Europe!

Really? Europe is at my doorstep. "Europe who?"

That's very rude! You're a poo!

2: Knock, knock.

"Where's there?"

Hawaii.

"Hawaii who?"

I'm quite fine thank you. Hawaii you?

3: Knock, knock.

"Where's there?"

Iran.

"Iran who?

Iran all the way here! Can I have something to drink?

4: Knock, knock.

"Where's there?"

Havana.

"Havana who?"

I'm Havana great time and I wish you were here!

5: Knock, knock.

"Where's there?"

Amarillo!

"Amarillo who?"

Amarillo nice guy! If you let me in, you'll see that.

6: Knock, knock.

"Where's there?"

Venice.

"Venice who?"

Venice your mother coming back, can we play until then?

7: Knock, knock.

"Where's there?"

Juneau.

"Juneau who?"

Juneau what the capital of Alaska is? I need to know for my homework.

8: Knock, knock.

"Where's there?"

Kenya.

"Kenya who?"

Kenya tell me where the key is so I can unlock the door?

9: Knock, knock.

"Where's there?"

Ida.

"Ida who?"

It's actually pronounced Idaho but nice try.

10: Knock, knock.

"Where's there?"

Jamaica!

"Jamaica who?"

Jamaica-ing a mistake. Let me in and we can talk about it.

11: Knock, knock.

"Where's there?"

Sherwood.

"Sherwood who?"

Sherwood like someone to open the door sometime soon.

12: Knock, knock.

"Where's there?"

Garden!

"Garden who?"

We're garden the treasure if you want to join us.

13: Knock, knock.

"Where's there?"

Alaska.

"Alaska who?"

This is the last time Alaska to open the door.

14: Knock, knock.

"Where's there?"

Avenue.

"Avenue who?"

Avenue heard me knock on this door before? You're pretending you don't know me, aren't you?

15: Knock, knock.

"Where's there?"

Europe!

"Europe who?"

Europe very early today!

16: Knock, knock.

"Where's there?"

Heaven.

"Heaven who?"

Heaven seen you in a long time! Open the door so we can catch up.

17: Knock, knock.

"Where's there?"

House!

"House who?"

House the family doing? I haven't seen you guys in a while.

18: Knock, knock.

"Who's there?"

Sherwood.

"Sherwood who?"

Sherwood be nice if we could talk inside the house.

19: Knock, knock.

"Where's there?"

Utah.

"Utah who?"

Utah one that told me to come over and now you don't know who I am!

20: Knock, knock.

"Where's there?"

Yukon.

"Yukon who?"

Yukon only know if you let me in first.

21: Knock, knock.

"Where's there?"

Hawaii.

"Hawaii who?"

Hawaii really messed up pizza with their pineapples.

22: Knock, knock.

"Who's there?"

New York.

"New York who?"

I New York door was locked so I knocked to let you know I was here.

23: Knock, knock.

"Who's there?"

Adair!

"Adair who?"

Adair you to move out of the doorway!

24: Knock, knock.

"Who's there?"

Africa.

"Africa who."

Africa love it when you open the door without asking questions.

25: Knock, knock.

"Who's there?"

Abyssinia.

"Abyssinia who?"

Abyssinia lot of people knocking on your door lately.

26: Knock, knock.

"Who's there?"

Alaska!

"Alaska who?"

Alaska questions around here!

Chapter Five: If a Dirty Dish Knocked on Your Door, Would You Wash it?

Jokes are better in the company of others! It's true. We laugh a whole lot more when we're around others than we would if we were by ourselves. In fact, we laugh up to 30 times more when we hear a joke with other people than if we heard the joke when we were alone. Maybe it's because laughter is contagious, or maybe you just hear the really good jokes when you're with others and the not so good jokes when you're alone.

1: Knock, knock.

Now this time we should say 'what's there.' Are you ready? "What's there?"

Dish.

"Dish who?"

Dish is a bad joke...sorry.

2: Knock, knock.

"What's there?"

Stopwatch!

"Stopwatch who?"

Stopwatch you are doing and come and play with me!

3: Knock, knock.

"What's there?"

Radio.

"Radio who?"

Radio not I'm coming in, so move out of the way.

4: Knock, knock.

"Who's there?"

Tissue.

"Tissue who?"

Tissue that I want to open the door.

5: Knock, knock.

"Who's there?"

Cargo.

"Cargo who?"

No! Owls go who, cars go beep.

6: Knock, knock.

"Who's there?"

Comb.

"Comb who?"

Comb down, open the door, and then I'll tell you.

7: Knock, knock.

"What's there?"

Ghosts go.

"Ghosts go who?"

I'm pretty sure ghosts go boo, not who.

8: Knock, knock.

"What's there?"

Dishes.

"Dishes who?"

Dishes not the best weather to be talking out on the doorstep.

9: Knock, knock.

"Who's there?"

From.

"From who?"

Technically, if you want to be grammatically correct, you should say "from whom."

10: Knock, knock.

"What's there?"

Wooden shoe.

"Wooden shoe who?"

Wooden shoe like to hear another joke first.

11: Knock, knock.

"What's there?"

Wire!

"Wire who?"

Wire you asking me so many questions? You're really nosey.

12: Knock, knock.

"Who's there?"

Thermos.

"Thermos who?"

Thermos be a better way to do this. I'm getting tired of knocking all the time.

13: Knock, knock.

"What's there?"

Leaf.

"Leaf who?"

Why can't you just leaf me alone!

14: Knock, knock.

"What's there?"

Pencil!

"Pencil who?"

I'm just a pencil, why would I have a last name?

15: Knock, knock.

"What's there?"

Dishes.

"Dishes who?"

Dishes my house!

16: Knock, knock.

"What's there?"

Irish!

"Irish who this time?"

Irish you would just let me in.

17: Knock, knock.

"What's there?"

Dozen.

"Dozen who?"

Dozen anyone know who I am?

18: Knock, knock.

"What's there?"

Hatch!

"Hatch who?"

God bless you!

19: Knock, knock.

"What's there?"

Fiddle!

"Fiddle who?"

Fiddle make you happy then I'll tell you, but you have to let me in first.

20: Knock, knock.

"What's there?"

The door.

"Wait! The door can talk?"

21: Knock, knock.

"What's there?"

Tank.

"Tank who?"

You're welcome!

22: Knock, knock.

"What's there?"

Needle.

"Needle who?"

Needle little help out here! Can you open the door and come help me?

23: Knock, knock.

"Who's there?"

Yacht!

"Yacht who?"

Yacht to know me by now. I've been knocking on your door forever.

24: Knock, knock.

"What's there?"

A door!

"A door who?"

A door between us there is. Open it up please. No, I'm not Yoda.

25: Knock, knock.

"What's there?"

Dishes.

"Dishes who?"

Dishes a really nice door. Is the other side of the door just as nice?

26: Knock, knock.

"What's there?"

C.D.

"C.D. who?"

C.D. person by your door? He wants to come inside the house.

27: Knock, knock.

"What's there?"

A broken pencil.

"A broken pencil who?"

It doesn't matter anymore. It's pointless.

28: Knock, knock.

"Who's there?"

Candy.

"Candy who?"

Candy door open or do I have to climb through the window?

29: Knock, knock.

"Who's there?"

Stopwatch!

"Stopwatch who?"

Stopwatch-ing T.V. and come play with me!

30: Knock, knock.

"Who's there?"

Police.

"Police who?"

Police leave the door open next time, so I don't have to knock.

31: Knock, knock.

"What's there?"

Bed!

"Bed who?"

I bed you can guess if you give it a try.

32: Knock, knock.

"What's there?"

Dumbbell.

"Dumbbell who?"

Your dumbbell doesn't work yet, so I'm knocking.

33: Knock, knock.

"Who's there?"

Razor!

"Razor who?"

Razor hands up and give me all your money!

34: Knock, knock.

"What's there?"

Canoe.

"Canoe who?"

Canoe help me open this door. I think it's locked.

35: Knock, knock.

"What's there?"

Comb.

"Comb who?"

Comb and open the door and I'll tell you.

36: Knock, knock.

"Who's there?"

Dishes.

Not again! "Dishes who?"

Dishes the police ma'am. I suggest you open the door right now.

37: Knock, knock.

"What's there?"

Fork!

"Fork who?"

Oh fork-get it! I'm leaving.

38: Knock, knock.

"What's there?"

Lock.

"Lock who?"

It's your door. Your door is locked. Unlock it please.

39: Knock, knock.

"What's there?"

Razor!

"Razor who?"

Razor hands in the air like you just don't care!

40: Knock, knock.

"What's there?"

Tennis.

"Tennis who?"

Tennis what you get when you add five to five. I'm the math teacher, by the way.

41: Knock, knock.

"What's there?"

Wooden shoe!

"Wooden shoe who?"

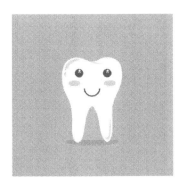

42: Knock, knock.

"What's there?"

Tooth.

"Tooth who?"

Tooth or dare is one of my favorite games!

Well, wooden shoe like to know. You'll have to open up first.

43: Knock, knock.

"What's there?"

Udder.

"Udder who?"

These jokes are udder madness! Wouldn't you agree?

44: Knock, knock.

"Who's there?"

Moustache!

"Moustache who?"

I moustache you a very important question, so let me in.

45: Knock, knock.

"Who's there?"

Letter.

"Letter who?"

You better letter in before she knocks down the door.

46: Knock, knock.

"Who's there?"

Java!

"Java who?"

Java dog? I swear I can hear one barking.

47: Knock, knock.

"What's there?"

Hula!

"Hula who?"

I like hula hooping too!

48: Knock, knock.

"Who's there?"

Wood!

"Wood who?"

Wood you be a dear and open up the door?

Chapter Six: Is it a Thing? Is it a Name? Is it a Place? Whatever it is, it's Funny.

People who laugh a lot live longer. I'm not kidding about that one. For every 15 minutes you laugh you make your life 2 days longer! Make sure you laugh a lot and make others laugh too. Maybe if we all laugh all the time we can live for a very long time!

1: Knock, knock.

"Who's there?"

Spell.

"Spell who?"

Okay, if you insist. W. H. O. There you go.

2: Knock, knock.

"Who's there?"

Boo!

"Boo who?"

Why are you crying? The joke wasn't that bad.

3: Knock, knock.

"Who's there?"

Armageddon!

"Armageddon who?"

Armageddon outta here before you ask any more questions.

4: Knock, knock.

"Who's there?"

Doctor.

"Doctor who?"

No, it's just the Doctor.

5: Knock, knock.

"Who's there?"

Toodle.

"Toodle who?"

Well toodle-loo to you, too!

6: Knock, knock.

"Who's there?"

Irish.

"Irish who?"

Irish you wouldn't ask me so many questions.

7: Knock, knock.

"Who's there?"

Police!

"Police who?"

What are you talking about? It's the police, open the door now!

8: Knock, knock.

"Who's there?"

To.

"To who?"

I believe the correct question is to whom.

9: Knock, knock.

"Who's there?"

Let's eat!

"Let's eat who?"

No one! You can't go around eating people.

10: Knock, knock.

"Who's there?"

Scold.

"Scold who?"

Scold out here, can I please come in?

11: Knock, knock.

"Who's there?"

Witch!

A witch! "Witch who?"

Witch way is the store? I want to buy some candy.

12: Knock, knock.

"Who's there?"

I. D. K.

"I.D.K who?"

No, I seriously don't know. I can't remember.

13: Knock, knock.

"Who's there?"

Snow.

"Snow who?"

Snow use asking me that question when you can just open the door and see for yourself.

14: Knock, knock.

"Who's there?"

Wa!

"Wa who?"

What's got you so excited?

15: Knock, knock.

"Who's there?"

Extraterrestrial.

"Extraterrestrial who?"

Well, there aren't a lot of us, so which one do you think I am? I mean, how many of us do you know?

16: Knock, knock.

"Who's there?"

Says!

"Says who?"

Says me!

17: Knock, knock.

"Who's there?"

Urine.

Ewe! Why is there Urine at the door? "Urine who?"

Urine in trouble if you don't open the door right now!

18: Knock, knock.

"Who's there?"

Ooze!

"Ooze who?"

Can I speak to the one ooze in charge?

19: Knock, knock.

"Who's there?"

Nobel.

"Nobel who?"

Nobel, is what you have, which is why I'm always knocking.

20: Knock, knock.

"Who's there?"

Twit.

"Twit who?"

Do you hear an owl?

21: Knock, knock.

"Who's there?"

Shocking.

"Shocking who?"

Shocking how you haven't opened the door yet.

22: Knock, knock.

"Who's there?"

Police!

"Police who?"

Police let me in. I'm asking so nicely.

23: Knock, knock.

"Who's there?"

Dozen!

"Dozen who?"

Dozen anyone in there want to let me in already?

24: Knock, knock.

"Who's there?"

Some.

"Some who?"

Somebody that wants to come in!

25: Knock, knock.

"Who's there?"

Passion!

"Passion who?"

I was passion by and though I'd stop by for a visit.

26: Knock, knock.

"Who's there?"

Icy.

"Icy who."

You should see me, unless you need your glasses to see or something.

27: Knock, knock.

"Who's there?"

Alien!

"Alien who?"

How many Aliens do you know!

28: Knock, knock.

"Who's there?"

Armageddon.

"Armageddon who?"

Armageddon bored out here!

29: Knock, knock.

"Who's there?"

Closure.

"Closure who?"

You should really close your mouth while eating, otherwise everyone will see you chew. Chewed up food doesn't look good.

30: Knock, knock.

"Who's there?"

Control freak.

"Control—"

This is the part where you say, "Control freak who." I wasn't sure if you were going to say it the right way.

31: Knock, knock.

"Who's there?"

Déjà vu.

"Déjà vu who?"

Knock, knock.

"Who's there?"

Déjà vu.

"Déjà vu who?" Wait haven't we been through this already?

32: Knock, knock.

"Who's there?"

Burglar!

"Burglar who?"

Burglars don't knock silly. I was joking.

33: Knock, knock.

"Who's there?"

F.B.I.

"F.B.I who?"

We'll be asking the questions, if you don't mind!

34: Knock, knock.

"Who's there?"

Yah.

"Yah who?"

I prefer to use Google, but you're entitled to your own opinion.

35: Knock, knock.

"Who's there?"

Witch!

"Witch who?"

How many witches do you know? I'm the one that flies the broom.

36: Knock, knock.

"Who's there?"

Pizza man.

"Pizza man who?"

It's the pizza man! Do you want your pizza or not?

37: Knock, knock.

"Who's there?"

Double!

"Double who?"

W!

38: Knock, knock.

"Who's there?"

Grub!

"Grub who?"

Grub the door handle and pull it towards you. That's how easy it is to open a door.

39: Knock, knock.

"Who's there?"

Horton hears a.

"Horton hears a who?"

That's what I was going to say! It's not nice to interrupt people.

40: Knock, knock.

"Who's there?"

Little old lady.

"Little old lady who?"

Wow! I didn't know you could yodel!

41: Knock, knock.

"Who's there?"

Ho-ho.

"Ho-ho who?"

You know it's not every nice to interrupt someone when they're trying to do a Santa impression. By the way, yours could use a little work.

42: Knock, knock.

"Who's there?"

Hey!

"Hey who?"

What do you mean hey who? I'm saying hey to you and the polite thing to do is say hey back.

43: Knock, knock.

"Who's there?"

Hand and stick.

"Hand and stick who?"

Hand over the money! This is a stick up.

44: Knock, knock.

"Who's there?"

Intruder!

An intruder! How did he get in? "Intruder who?"

Intruder window!

45: Knock, knock.

"Who's there?"

Me!

"Me who?"

Sorry I don't speak Chinese. I must be at the wrong house.

46: Why did Sarah fall off of her swing?

"Why?"

Because she had no arms!

Knock, knock.

"Who's there?"

Not Sarah, that's for sure.

47: Knock, knock.

"Who's there?"

A little boy.

"A little boy who?"

A little boy who's too short to reach the doorbell, so I had to knock.

48: Knock, knock.

"Who's there?"

Noise.

"Noise who?"

Noise to meet you, too!

49: Knock, knock.

"Who's there?"

Nose!

"Nose who?"

Who nose?

50: Knock, knock.

"Who's there?"

Riot!

"Riot who?"

I'm riot on time so let me in.

51: Knock, knock.

"Who's there?"

Sorry.

"Sorry who?"

Sorry this is the wrong door.

52: Knock, knock.

"Who's there?"

Woo!

"Woo who?"

I know I'm excited too!

53: Knock, knock.

"Who's there?"

Such a!

"Such a who?"

Such a lot of questions! Are you a detective or something?

54: Knock, knock.

"Who's there?"

Snow.

"Snow who?"

Snow-body important! Maybe I'm the snowman from down the street. It's snow use though. I don't remember.

55: Knock, knock.

"Who's there?"

Not a doorbell!

56: Knock, knock.

"Who's there?"

U. C. I.

"U. C. I. who?"

UCI couldn't ring the doorbell and so I was forced to knock.

57: Knock, knock.

"Who's there?"

Moustache.

"Is this about that question you wanted to ask me?"

No, I'll shave it for later.

58: Knock, knock.

"Who's there?"

Woo.

"Woo who?"

Calm down. Why are you so excited?

59: Knock, knock.

"Who's there?"

I am.

"I am who?"

So, you don't know who you are either.

60: Knock, knock.

"Who's there?"

A Mayan.

"A Mayan who?"

A Mayan the way. If I am, then I'll move as soon as you open the door.

61: Knock, knock.

"Who's there?"

Weight king.

"Weight king who?"

I've been weight king for you to open this door for ages now.

62: Knock, knock.

"Who's there?"

Voodoo.

"Voodoo who?"

Voodoo you think you are speaking to? I guess you don't know, so that's why you asked.

63: Knock, knock.

"Who's there?"

Cook!

"Cook who?"

Yes, you are cuckoo, but so am I.

64: Knock, knock.

"Who's there?"

A fake noodle!

"A fake noodle who?"

Well, if you really want to know. People call me an impasta!

65: Knock, knock.

"Who's there?"

Hada.

"Hada who?"

I had a really good time. It's probably better next time if you actually let me in.

66: Knock, knock.

"Who's there?"

Stupid.

"Stupid who?"

I'd prefer not to answer that question.

67: Knock, knock.

"Who's there?"

Uncomfortable.

"Uncomfortable who?"

.....

68: Knock, knock.

"Who's there?"

Boo!

"AAAAHHH!"

It wasn't that scary.

69: Knock, knock.

"Who's there?"

Deaf.

"Deaf who?"

What did you say?

70: Knock, knock.

"Who's there?"

Spell.

"Spell who?"

If you're not careful, I'll cast one on you.

71: Will you remember me in a year?

Yes.

Will you remember me in a month?

Yes.

Will you remember me in a week?

Yes.

Will you remember me tomorrow?

Yes.

Knock, knock.

"Who's there?"

I thought you said you would remember me!

72: Knock, knock.

"Who's there?

An interrupting pirate.

"An interrupting—"

ARRRR!

73: Knock, knock.

"Who's there?"

Voodoo.

"Voodoo who?"

Voodoo you think!

74: Knock, knock.

"Who's there?"

Shhhh.

"Shhhh who?"

I told you to shhhh, why are you still talking?

75: Knock, knock.

"Who's there?"

Art!

"Art who?"

Art 2-D2

76: Knock, knock.

"Who's there?"

The door is open, you can see who's there.

77: Knock, knock.

"Who's there?"

Suspense.

"Suspense who?"

....

78: Knock, knock.

"Who's there?"

Yule.

"Yule who?"

Yule only know if you open the door and have a look.

Chapter Seven: It's a Joke but it Doesn't Come With a Door.

Did you know that children laugh more than adults? I guess children are funnier than adults as well. They know all the best jokes! Children laugh three times more than adults too, but that's because there's so much to laugh about. Animals laugh too, you know. Go outside and tell a bird a joke or two and you'll see they laugh just like you and me.

1: Cinderella is very bad at soccer. Do you know why?

Because she runs away from the ball!

2: Where would a cow go to have fun?

To the moo-vies!

3: Why did the bicycle fall over?

Because it was two-tired!

4: Seagulls fly over the sea, so what flies over the bay?

Bagels!

5: How do you make a tissue dance?

By putting some boogie in it!

6: A room that doesn't have doors or windows is called a what?

A mushroom!

7: Which hand should you write with?

Neither hand, you should write with a pencil!

8: What animal loves a good baseball game?

A bat!

9: What did the snowman say to the other snowman?

Do you smell carrots?

10: What is a vehicle with four wheels and flies called?

A garbage truck!

11: Why did I throw butter out the window?

I wanted to see a butterfly!

12: A key that opens a banana is called a what?

A monkey!

13: Where's the best place to get a pencil?

Pennsylvania!

14: Why did the broom show up late for work?

Because it over-swept!

15: Why don't teddy bears eat a lot?

Because they're always stuffed!

16: Why would you bury your flashlight?

Because the batteries are dead!

17: Which letter in the alphabet is filled with the most water?

The C!

18: Which of the months in the year have 28 days?

All of them, silly!

19: When is a door no longer a door?

When it is ajar!

20: What kind of tree will you find in your hand?

A palm!

21: Why do lions eat all their food raw?

Because they don't know how to cook!

22: Why did a bee hum?

Because it didn't know the words to the song!

23: What does a lazy dog do for fun?

It would chase a parked car!

24: What is the last thing I took off before I went to bed?

I took my feet off the ground!

25: What do you call a stinky fairy?

Stinkerbell!

26: What did the gum say to the underside of the shoe?

I'm think I'm stuck on you!

27: How can you cure dandruff?

By being bald!

28: What does the invisible man drink?

Evaporated milk!

29: why should you never play basketball with a pig?

Because he'll hog the ball!

30: What will you get if you steal a calendar?

12 months!

31: What can you say about the new restaurant on the moon?

It's out of this world!

32: Why can't your nose be 12 inches long?

Because then it would be a foot!

33: Why should you put honey under your pillow?

So you can have sweet dreams!

34: How can you stop an astronaut's baby from crying all the time?

You should rocket!

35: Why can't ghosts lie?

Because everyone sees right through them!

36: Why is a math book always sad?

Because it has a lot of problems!

37: Why did they arrest the picture?

Because he was framed!

38: Why would the skeleton not cross the road?

Because he had no guts!

39: What would a spider wear on her wedding day?

A webbing dress!

40: What insect is good at spelling?

A spelling bee!

41: Why didn't the skeleton go to the dance?

Because he had nobody to go with!

42: How would the ocean say hello to the beach?

It would wave!

43: Why did the chicken cross the road?

We cannot guess what a chicken could be thinking!

44: How do you know when the moon has had enough to eat?

When it's full!

45: Why would a golfer wear two pairs of pants?

Just in case he got a hole in one!

46: What shoes does a spy wear?

Sneakers!

47: What time would it be if a monster came to school?

Time to run away!

48: What time is it when an elephant sits on your car?

Time to get a new car!

49: When should you take your computer to a doctor?

When it has a virus!

50: What can you catch but never hold or throw?

A cold!

51: What would get wet while it's drying?

A towel!

52: What kind of underwear does a cloud wear?

Thunderwear!

53: What did the volcano say to his best friend?

I lava you!

54: What does a duck use its tail feathers for?

To cover its buttquack!

55: Why can't you tell a joke to a glass?

Because it would crack it up!

56: How do signs talk to each other?

With sign language!

57: Why are jokes about pizza not good?

Because they're too cheesy!

58: What subject in school is a snake good at?

Hiss-tory!

59: Learning how to pick up trash isn't hard.

You just have to pick it up as you go along.

60: What do you get when you cross a vampire with a snowman?

You get frostbite!

61: Where would you find a dog with no legs?

Exactly where you last left him!

62: Why did the cookie go to the hospital?

Because he felt crummy!

63: Where would you find a vampire that writes books?

Pennsylvania!

64: What did Jack say to Jill at the bottom of the hill?

I spilled the water!

65: What's green and smells like yellow paint?

Green paint!

66: What time is it when a ball hits you on the head?

Time to go to the hospital!

67: What do you call a berry that is sad?

A blueberry!

68: Don't give a balloon to Elsa.

She'll just let it go!

69: What happened to the kidnapping in the park?

Well, they had to wake him up.

70: Why will you never catch an elephant hiding in a tree?

Because they're just really good at it.

71: I spent at least five minutes fixing that clock.

I think it was five minutes. I can't be sure because the clock was broken.

72: What do you call a pea that's tired?

Very sleep-pea.

73: What did the elevator say to the ground floor?

I think I'm coming down with something.

74: You should never trust an atom.

They make up everything!

75: What did the shark think after he ate a clown fish?

It tastes kind of funny to me.

76: Which fish is the most expensive?

A gold fish of course!

78: What is brown and can be quite sticky?

It's a stick!

79: What do you call someone that doesn't like math?

A calcu-hater!

80: You throw two rocks down into a valley and they say one thing to each other on the way down. What do they say?

The one says, "Ahhhhh!" While the other simple states, "I'm falling!" There isn't much else two rocks falling down a valley can say to each other.

81: Is it better if you paint with your right hand or with your left hand?

It's actually better if you paint with a paint brush, unless you're finger painting.

82: What do you say to someone who is trying to steal your cheese?

"That's nacho cheese!"

83: Where do all of the fish like to keep their hard earned money?

In the river bank of course!

84: What goes up but never comes down?

Your age, silly!

85: What did the baby corn ask the mama corn when they went out for a walk?

They asked, "Is popcorn coming with?"

86: Why do lions hate eating clowns?

Because they taste funny!

87: Where does a dog's Christmas presents come from?

They come from Santa Paws of course.

88: What would happen if a shark became really famous?

He would turn into a starfish!

89: Bananas peel easily.

That's why they have to put on lots of sunscreen before they go to the beach.

90: Knights are supposed to be brave and fearless. What happens when one of the knights is scared of the dark?

They just need to turn on the knight-light.

91: What time does a duck get out of bed?

As early as the quack of dawn!

92: Two tomatoes were racing each other. What did the fast tomato say to the slower tomato?

It said, "You need to ketchup!"

93: Why do fish prefer to live in saltwater?

Because pepper water would make them sneeze too much!

94: That pig knows karate! What should we call him?

A pork chop!

95: What do you call a fish that has no eyes?

A fsh.

96: What has to be broken before it can be used and is really tasty?

An egg!

97: Which of the tires on a car won't move if you turn the car?

The spare tire, silly!

98: We hired a pony to sing 'Happy Birthday' at a little girl's party, but when it got there it couldn't sing at all. Why not?

Because it was just a little hoarse!

99: What did the buffalo dad say to his son when he left for school early in the morning?

He said, "Bison!"

100: What kind of money do vampires like to use?

Blood money of course!

101: How would a comedian make a grumpy octopus laugh?

He would have to use ten-tickles!

102: Why are a guitar and a fish so different?

Because you can tune a guitar but you can't tuna fish!

103: What did the traffic light say to the cars in front of it?

It said, "Please turn around, I'm changing."

104: What are you supposed to do when a bull is charging you?

You should pay the bull of course!

105: Why was the number 6 afraid of the number 7?

Because number 6 heard that 7, 8, 9!

106: Why did the little boy eat his homework before coming to school?

Because the teacher told him that it would be a piece of cake!

107: What did the piece of paper say to the newly sharpened pencil?

It said, "Write on!"

108: What name would you give to a blind dinosaur?

I think we should call it a do-you-think-he-saurus!

109: Today I was at the bank and an old lady asked me to check her balance.

So, I pushed her over!

110: Did you hear about the man who is afraid of negative numbers?

He'll stop at nothing in order to avoid them!

Made in the USA
Middletown, DE
18 December 2022

19341391R00102